Welcome to
Friends and Family

What can you do with
your friends and family?
Read along and
have some fun!

Talk About It!

Friends and Family

Is a pet a part of your family? Here are some pets that kids have.

What makes a pet a good friend?

Word Bank

Here are some words that you may hear or read this week:

closet

monster

scared (adj.)

camping

outdoors

pack (v.)

ready

seed

soil

finally

Steck-Vaughn

READING STUDIO WEEKLY

Friends and Family

Level B Issue 5

Contents

In This Issue

Photo Acknowledgements

PP.9,10,11 John Williams; pp.12,13 Ken O'Donoghue.

Additional photography by Blend Image Photography Royalty Free/Veer; Comstock Royalty Free; Digital Vision Royalty Free; EyeWire Royalty Free; Photos.com Royalty Free; Photodisc/Getty Images Royalty Free; Stockbyte Royalty Free, Royalty-Free/CORBIS and the HA Collection.

ISBN 1-4190-2055-2

Printed in China

1 2 3 4 5 6 7 8 985 12 11 10 09 08 07 06 05

Language Builder

Thank You, Aunt Sue

Dear Aunt Sue,

I had a good time at your house. I liked cooking **outdoors** in your *yard*. It was fun getting the *corn* **ready** to eat.

I like your pet *lizard*. But Mom does not like lizards. She is **scared** of them.

Next time I will **pack** my tent. We could sleep under the *stars*. Thank you for everything.

Love,

Jen

Sam and Bob

One night something woke up Sam.
A little monster stood by him.

"I am going to live under your bed,"
it said.

Sam said, "You will be cold there.
You can live in my closet."

Sam and the monster became friends.
Sam named the monster Bob. Bob helped
Sam with his homework.

It was nice to have Bob as a friend.
Bob played games with Sam.

Sam's friend Dan came to stay one night.
"What did I hear?" Dan asked.
"Is something under your bed?"

Sam said, "Nothing is under my bed.
But my monster is in the closet."

"M-m-monster?" asked Dan.

Sam said, "Don't be scared.
You can meet him! His name is Bob."

Our Camping Trip

We went camping with my dad. I helped Dad pack the car. My sister helped, too.

tent: place to stay made of cloth and held up by poles

We found a good place to camp. I helped Dad put up the **tent**. My sister helped, too.

We played outside. Dad and I played with the kite. My sister played, too.

We cooked dinner outdoors. I helped Dad cook our food. My sister helped, too.

We went to bed in our sleeping bags.
I helped Dad get things ready for bed.
My sister helped, too.

Our camping trip was fun!

Planting and Growing

My friends and I are going to grow beans at school. We need seeds. What else do we need?

We need seeds and soil. What else do we need?

We need seeds, soil, and a pot. My dad helps me buy what I need.

How can I help my bean seeds grow?

First I put soil into the pot.

Then I dig a hole with my finger. I put the seeds in the hole.

Next I put soil on the seeds. I water them.

Finally, I put the seeds in the sun.

The soil, water, and sun will help the seeds grow into beans.

My Turn to Write

My Day Away from Home

Think about a time that you stayed with friends or family. Who did you stay with? What did you do? Write your journal entry on pages 96 and 97 of your Studio Log.

Your notes may look like this.

Where
Juan's house

People
Juan
his mom
his dad

What we did
ate dinner
played games
went to bed in sleeping bags

Your journal may look like this.

June 11, 2006
I stayed with my friend Juan. His mom and dad are very nice. We ate dinner. Then we played games. We went to bed in sleeping bags. I would like to go back to his house some day.

Fluency

Pets Are Our Friends

Lots of people have dogs. Some people have cats. Some people choose other pets. They choose animals like snakes and lizards.

Cats and dogs make good pets. They like to be around people. Snakes and lizards can be good pets, too.

You can get a snake or lizard from a pet store. Snakes and lizards need special care. You need to talk to an animal doctor before you get one. The animal doctor can tell you how to care for a snake or lizard.

Project

A Family Portrait

A family portrait is a picture of all the family together. Draw a picture of your family. Tell who each person is. Don't forget the family pets! Turn to page 98 in your Studio Log.

Steck-Vaughn
A Harcourt Achieve Imprint

Steck-Vaughn Summer Studio Reading

ISBN 1-4190-2055-2
9 781419 020551
90000